Forex Trading for Beginners:

Everything You Should Know Before Getting Into This Business

By

Paul Serafin

The follow book is reproduced below with the goal of providing information that is as accurate and reliable as possible. Regardless, purchasing this book can be seen as consent to the fact that both the publisher and the author of this book are in no way experts on the topics discussed within and that any recommendations or suggestions that are made herein are for entertainment purposes only. Professionals should be consulted as needed prior to undertaking any of the action endorsed herein.

This declaration is deemed fair and valid by both the American Bar Association and the Committee of Publishers Association and is legally binding throughout the United States.

Furthermore, the transmission, duplication or reproduction of any of the following work including specific information will be considered an illegal act irrespective of if it is done electronically or in print. This extends to creating a secondary or tertiary copy of the work or a recorded copy and is only allowed with express written consent from the Publisher. All additional right reserved.

The information in the following pages is broadly considered to be a truthful and accurate account of facts and as such any inattention, use or misuse of the information in question by the reader will render any resulting actions solely under their purview. There are no scenarios in which the publisher or the original author of this work can be in any fashion deemed liable for any hardship or damages that may befall them after undertaking information described herein.

Additionally, the information in the following pages is intended only for informational purposes and should thus be thought of as universal. As befitting its nature, it is presented without assurance regarding its prolonged validity or interim quality. Trademarks that are mentioned are done without written consent and can in no way be considered an endorsement from the trademark holder.

Table of Contents

Introduction 1

Chapter 1: Introduction to Forex trading 3

Chapter 2: The Forex market landscape 7

Chapter 3: Know the terminology 13

Chapter 4: Getting started 21

Chapter 5: Trading styles and strategies 25

Chapter 6: Choosing a forex broker - step-by-step guide 43

Chapter 7: The purpose of demo accounts 47

Chapter 8: Step by Step Guide for Opening your First Live Forex Trading Position 53

Chapter 9: Risk management – How to minimize risk and maximize rewards 57

Chapter 10: The important role of Forex research 61

Conclusion 63

Description 67

Introduction

Congratulations on purchasing *Forex Trading for Beginners* and thank you for doing so.

The following chapters will discuss the dynamic landscape that is the foreign exchange market, essential terminology and concepts beginner traders need to be familiar with, commonly used trading strategies and how to develop one's own, the different trading styles, trading tools and indicators, risk management strategies to keep losses at the minimum level, an overview and step-by-step guide to demo accounts as well as how to open a live account. Due to the critical role information-gathering plays in trading, a section that discusses the importance of research, and why it is needed, is included at the end.

Successful trading in Forex begins by knowing the basics. The trillions of US dollars in currency trading that take place each day is a good motivator to investigate a venture into this lucrative market. This market is open and accessible to all which means that armed with adequate knowledge and tools there is no reason why you should not join the countless of other successful Forex traders in reaping the spoils. That there is plenty of profit to be earned in Forex is without doubt, what is often undervalued, though, is the necessary knowledge required. You have to commit to learning and educating yourself continuously about currencies and the currency market. You've taken the right step in this direction by reading this book.

There are plenty of books on this subject on the market, thanks again for choosing this one! Every effort was made to ensure it is full of as much useful information as possible, please enjoy!

Chapter 1
Introduction to Forex trading

Why choose Forex trading?

Forex trading, also known as currency trading is one of the more exciting speculative online trading opportunities to make money. As a currency trader, the nature of your trade involves buying and selling currency pairs resulting in either profit or loss.

Like you would start and grow any other type of business, Forex trading requires commitment, knowledge and a steady investment of time to practice trading in pursuit of finding perfect winning strategies. But this is not all. You also need to be business-minded and patient. Forex trading is not the option if you are looking for a quick-fix solution to earning big money fast. In order to be a successful Forex trader, you will have to work as hard as you would at starting any other business.

Benefits of being a Forex trader

There are numerous reasons to engage in Forex trading. Some of the benefits include:

1. Convenience

    Forex trading is conducted online and with a suitable computer the market can be accessed from wherever you are in the world. This global market is open for trade 24-hours a day, across international time zones, Monday through to

Friday. The high volumes of forex traded every day create a demand, enabling you to buy and sell in your desired currency pairs.

2. Easily accessible to a beginner

   One of the popular reasons beginners choose the Forex market is that it is relatively simple to set up and start your first trade. Once you are ready and have selected the right broker to help you succeed at your goals, you fund your account with a low deposit. You can make your first trade in as little as a few minutes (it is highly recommended that you practice as much as possible on demo accounts before trading live).

3. Multiple trading styles and strategies to try out and implement

   Fortunately, there are many styles and strategies with which to approach Forex trading. Your job is to find the best one for your personality and risk profile.

4. Various risk management techniques to lower loss

   There are a number of techniques to include in your trade plan to lower your position's vulnerability to risk. From implementing Stop-Loss orders to asking for a lower leverage ratio, you can trade with a certain amount of confidence and enjoy protection against major losses.

If you'd like to progress from a beginner trader to professional status, it is important you begin by setting reasonable goals that you work hard to accomplish. One such goal could be earning a profit at the end of your first month. It does not matter if the profit attained is big or small. The problem with having unrealistic goals is that they may lead you to taking huge unnecessary risks in your trade position with the end result being undesired losses. This is a guaranteed way to end your hopes of building wealth through Forex trading quickly.

Think Forex trading is for you? Here are important questions to ask yourself before you delve deeper into becoming the next top Forex trader:

1. What are your Forex trade goals?
2. Are these goals realistic?
3. Do you know what your risk appetite is?
4. Do you have money available you are willing to lose?
5. Do you have the time and necessary patience to try out different strategies before finding the one that works for you?
6. Are you prepared for initial setbacks, challenges and losses?
7. How will you handle these challenges?
8. How will you handle wins?

One last note: Loss is not failure; it is a path to learning from and building on experience. It is the path every beginner must be prepared to walk on. Equally important is how you handle wins and what you do with profits earned.

Chapter 2

The Forex market landscape

By familiarizing yourself with the nature of Forex trading you can establish a firm footing into the Forex world. The first characteristic to understand and accept is that exposure to risk is part and parcel of Forex trading.

One of the reasons why the Forex market is so exciting to participate in is due to it being a dynamic one. Its constantly changing nature is influenced by real-time events, many of which are unpredictable.

The Foreign exchange market has many influencers, among the more common are: inflation and interest rate changes, a country's Balance of Payments status, international current affairs, political events and even natural/geographical events. The constant movement and multiple factors affecting foreign exchange rates give rise to volatility which is a prerequisite to high profit opportunities.

The nature and role of risk in the Forex market

As a novice who has decided to dip one's toe in currency trading, it is important to understand one of the fundamentals of forex trading - the risk factor. Your primary goal is to make a profit and minimizing risk is the key to unlocking the door to success. Risk can be controlled through a number of control measures that are implemented. A whole chapter is dedicated to risk management techniques.

As a beginner, it highly recommended that you determine beforehand the amount you are willing to lose and stand firm not to risk more than this. It is also advisable that you start off with a minimal trading investment amount and to increase its value as your experience and confidence in Forex trading grows.

Who are the players in Forex trading?

It is a good starting point to know all the important participants involved in Forex trading as it provides a better understanding of just how dynamic this market really is. Right at the top of this list is the central bank of each country (Federal Reserve, Bank of England, European Central Bank, etc.) that represents the government and oversees their monetary policies – one of which is determining interest rates (a determinant of market movement).

Next, down the line is the inter-bank market made up of the largest banks in the world. A few familiar names are Barclays, HSBC and Citi bank. These larger banks have well-established credit relationships with each other which are favorable for allowing competitive foreign exchange pricing. These banks also conduct an immeasurable amount of foreign exchange transactions daily which makes the inter-bank a serious player.

The Forex market also has smaller participants such as large commercial companies, hedges and speculators - that would be you.

Major Foreign exchange currencies to know

Every beginner trader wanting to speculate in the Forex market should become familiar with the 8 major currencies that are traded:

1. USD – U.S. dollar
2. GBP – British pound
3. JPY – Japanese yen
4. EUR – European euro
5. CHF – Swiss franc
6. AUD – Australian dollar
7. NZD - New Zealand dollar
8. CAD – Canadian dollar

You can also buy and sell in numerous other currencies – called cross currencies – against the US Dollar.

When can Forex trading be conducted?

You can buy and sell currencies from anywhere in the world (as it is conducted online) and at any time. The fact that it offers round-the-clock trading times is one of its main attractive features. You have full control of your activities and can access them 24/7. You can monitor your trades, change the terms of your open deals, close trades, or should you wish, withdraw profits.

Seeing that the Forex market is a global one, trading in foreign currency can be done 24 hours, five days a week. The currency market opens for trading Monday morning in Sydney, Australia and closes Friday evening in New York, USA.

Best times to trade

The best time to trade in Forex is during high volatility but a trader can't track market movements every minute in a 24-hour timeframe. Fortunately, there are trade sessions that offer the best times to trade. These are:

- The Asian Session (7 pm – 4 am EST)

  Even though this is not a volatile session as some of the other sessions can prove to be, traders can enjoy a good performance. The USD/JPY currency pair is generally successful for this session.

- The European Session (2 am – 12 pm EST)

  Generally regarded as one of the more beneficial sessions in which to trade Forex due to the number of large commercial banks found in London, most of the major currency transactions are made during the duration of this session. It is a favorable time period to use a good trade strategy using any combination of currency pairing.

- The U.S. Session (8 am – 5 pm EST)

    Another encouraging session in which to implement trade strategies successfully as there is good cause for advantageous intraday swings and decent volatility on the desired currency pair of your choosing is the US trading session.

The U.S. session is run concurrently (between 8 am and 12 pm EST) to the European session. Trade during this time offers good volatility as much of the world's economic releases are made during this session.

The role of volatility in Forex trading

It is understandable for novice traders to be wary of the term 'volatility'. It is a word that is, after all, associated with unpredictability and uncertainty. How can you prepare for the unforeseeable?

In Forex trading volatility has its use and traders can take advantage of a volatile market. A volatile market creates opportunities that encourage either buying or selling of foreign currencies. A stagnant market offers no openings to make a profit.

Chapter 3

Know the terminology

In order to trade successfully in the Forex market, you need to have a solid grasp of some of the terminology used. Forex trading has its own language so to speak due to the large body of terms and concepts used. As a beginner trader, it is of the utmost importance that you become familiar with these terms or else you make trading practically impossible. Some of the basic concepts include:

Currency Pairs

A Forex trade is made up of the buying/selling of two currencies. Using the example of EUR/JPY, the first currency – EUR is referred to as the base currency and the second – JPY refers to the quote currency.

Exchange Rate

The exchange rate is the rate at which you buy/sell one currency for another. The exchange rate indicates how much of the quote currency (the second currency) you need in order to buy 1 unit of the base currency (first currency).

In this currency pair example: USD/JPY = 1.4110, 1 U.S. dollar will cost you 1.4110 Japanese yen.

Quote

A quote refers to the market price that is always represented by 2 figures. For example: 1.33488 (bid/selling price) / 1.13345 (ask/buying price).

Ask Price

The Ask price or offer price is the price indicated on the right-hand side of a Forex trade quote. It is the price value at which you can purchase the base currency.

For example, if in this currency pair - JPY/EUR the quote is 1.1945/1.1987, you can purchase 1 yen for 1.1987 euros.

Bid Price

The bid price is the amount at which you can sell a currency pair.

In this example – the EUR/GBP currency pair is quoted at 1.5568/1.5570, the euro is the bid price at which you can sell the currency pair.

You will notice that the bid price is always of lower value than ask.

Pip

One of the most basic terms novice traders need to understand is Pip. This is a unit of measurement that relates to the movement in the exchange rate. Pip stands for 'percentage in point'.

Ultimately Pip offers a numeric value that determines profit and loss. A single pip has a value of 0.0001.

As a trader, you will reference profit and loss or changes in currencies value in pips. For example, having made a profit, you would say, "My last trade earned me 10 pips". In referring to change in movement, you would say, "the USD/JPY lost 10 pips between this session and the last".

Spread

In simple terms, Spread refers to the price you pay for making a trade, or in other terms, what your broker charges you for their service. In determining spread, you find the difference between the Bid price from the Ask price.

Brokers usually offer fixed spreads and variable spreads. Fixed spreads are not influenced by market factors and reserve the same amount of pips in relation to the ask and bid price. Variable spreads can increase or decrease according to the movements and activity in the Forex market. Spreads quoted can vary between broker firms so doing your research is vital.

Leverage

Forex brokers offer their traders a 'loan amount' for every trade position. This is to allow traders access to more trading capital. Leverage refers to the quantitative correlation of the lending margin. Leverage can present both an advantage (used to earn greater profits) or a disadvantage (experience substantial losses) and traders are therefore urged to consider the leverage offered carefully.

Each trader's exposure to risk (making a profit or loss) differs and is relevant to the leverage ratios they are offered. A higher leverage offers the opportunity to make greater profits or major losses while with a lower leverage ratio any gains will be relatively lower and any losses less acute.

Lot

Forex is transacted in amounts referred to as lots. A standard lot equals 100,000 units of the base currency in a currency pair. A micro lot equals 1,000 units.

In this example - EUR/USD at 1.5525, you buy 1 standard lot of 100,000 Euros and you sell 155,250 US dollars. Likewise, when you sell 1 micro lot of EUR/USD at 1.3320, you sell 1,000 Euros and you buy 1,332. US dollars.

Margins

A Forex trader requires a margin (minimum amount of funds) in order to trade. A margin refers to the minimum amount or deposit required to open or maintain an open position. This margin allows you effectively take a 'loan' – access to a larger amount of capital.

If your trade is based on a 1% margin, you will need for every 100 USD 100 that you trade with, a deposit of USD 1. If you wish to buy 1 standard lot (i.e. 100,000 of USD/EUR), you need to uphold a margin of only 1% of the traded amount in your account - USD 1,000. Wait a minute you say. How do you buy 100,000 USD/EUR if you have only USD 1,000? This is where margin trading or borrowed capital comes into play. Forex brokers offer traders a loan amount with which to trade referred to as margin trading.

Margin call

A margin call is a warning alert you receive when you do not have sufficient funds in your trading account with which to engage in, in open trades. This occurs when your floating losses exceed the lowest margin amount required. Margin calls form part of an effective risk management strategy.

Position

A position is a trade held open for any length of time, from a few hours to days, weeks, months and even years.

Long Position

When you trade a long position, you make a decision to buy a base currency. One reason to trade a long position is that you speculate a currency will increase in value in relation to another currency.

Short Position

When you trade a short position, you opt to sell a base currency. One reason to trade a short position is when you believe the currency's value will fall in relation to another and you hope the sell will gain you profit.

Various Order Types

There are different types of Orders that are applicable to a Forex trade. These are:

Entry Order

An Entry order is an order to purchase or sell currency immediately at the current market price.

Open Order

An Open order is an order to buy/sell currency, stocks, or commodities (oil, gold, silver, etc.) that remains open until you opt to close it.

Limit Order

A Limit order is an order that trades in currency at a price limit that you determine. For example, if the current market price for USD/GBP is at 1.45 you place a sell order when the currency pair price reaches 1.46. The sell limit order is set more than the market price and the buy limit order is set when the limit order is lower than the current price.

Stop-entry Order

A Stop-entry order is given when you opt to buy a currency that is more than the given market price or sell currency lower than the market price if you believe the market price will carry on in its current direction.

Take Profit Order (TP)

This type of order closes your trade position when it has attained a specific level of profit.

Stop-Loss Order (SL)

You can place a Stop-Loss order to close your trade position when it has suffered a specific level of loss (the amount you are willing to lose). This is one of the top risk-reducing strategies that minimizes your loss and protects your capital.

Stop-loss orders can be set with automated trading software so that you don't need to watch the markets 24-hours a day. The software will implement this strategy on your behalf automatically.

Liquidity

Liquidity is a term that makes reference to the level of activity in the trade market. Level of activity is established by taking into account factors such as the number of traders engaged in buying and selling and the quantity of trade value involved. The high level of liquidity in the Forex market is due its round-the-clock trading times Monday to Friday and the fact that it generates high volumes of revenue – approximately $6 trillion daily.

Volatility

Volatility is the calculated measure of the extreme changes in currency market prices. Volatility is directly influenced by liquidity. Low liquidity, higher volatility, and vice versa. More active traders in a session result in slight changes up and down.

Chapter 4

Getting started

How a basic Forex trade is made

In a Forex transaction, you don't really buy the actual currency which means that it does not get dropped it into your trading account. Basically, Forex trading involves you speculating on the currency exchange rate. You assess the direction the exchange rate will move, and you enter an agreement (contract-based) with your Forex broker, based on your speculation, to be paid by your broker or you pay your broker (dependent on how right or wrong your speculation was).

Before you can make your first trade you will have to open your trading account with a deposit amount (more on this later). Remember you don't have to supply the full amount of funds need for your transaction. You have access to borrowed funds in the form of a leverage ratio provided by your broker. This ratio has to be agreeable to you as it has implied financial consequences. This leverage ratio ties in with the profit and loss of your trade so consider it carefully. As a beginner, you may want to proceed with caution and opt for a lower leverage ratio, to begin with. With more experience (and hopefully higher profit margins) you can increase the leverage ratio.

You buy and sell currencies in a pair.

Using the British Pound/Dollar (GBP/USD) example the first currency in the pair is the GBP is the base currency. The second, USD, is the counter currency. When you buy, you buy the base currency in the pair and sell the counter currency. When you sell, you sell the base and buy the counter currency.

How leverage is used in a trade

You open a trading account with a deposit of $1,000. The trade position you want to engage in requires a price tag of $500,000. How do you make up the difference? You are offered and accept a leverage of 1:100. Your broker puts up the remainder of the funds - $495,000.

Any profits gained from the transaction are deposited into your account and losses are deducted from your account balance.

Traders can make use of a number of risk management techniques to protect their capital from loss. Remember to ask your broker what techniques they offer (in addition to you implementing your own) to protect your money.

A no negative balance protection ensures that your losses will never go beyond the funds you have in your account. If you suffer a loss that reaches your capital balance, the trade position is automatically closed so that your account does not result in a negative balance.

Executing an order

The process of completing an order is referred to as execution. To initiate the execution of a trade you send your broker an order who then makes a decision to fill, reject or re-quote the order. If it is filled a notification is sent to you confirming this. The prompt execution of a trade order is critical as any delay on the part of your broker has the potential to lose you money. The Forex market is dynamic as well as fast-paced and if your chosen broker does not fill orders in the appropriate time, this can spell disaster for you.

How is a profit made in Forex trading?

In buying and selling currencies profit is made when you correctly work out whether one currency (in a currency pairing) will strengthen or weaken in relation to the other currency in the pair. The key factor to profit making is to buy when a currency price is low and when its value has risen, to sell.

Currency price fluctuations are influenced by numerous factors such as supply and demand, economic monetary policies and political factors to even natural disasters. One of the disastrous consequences of the earthquake that took place in Japan in 2011 was the adverse effect it had on the price of the Japanese Yen.

In order to make money from Forex trading, a trader such as yourself needs to respond promptly to what is moving the markets. A trader reacts by using all the information at his/her disposal: news updates, examining and analyzing charts and other Forex tools. You must embrace constantly learning and evolving.

Chapter 5

Trading styles and strategies

Trading styles

Success in Forex trading is dependent on your trading style and strategies that you choose to engage in. As a beginner trader, you will want to find the ideal trading style to suit you.

The time frame involved in the different trading styles is a key factor in determining the best style for you. Trading styles can offer short term trade positions (scalping) to medium term (example swing trade) to long-term (trend trading) situated on the farthest end of the time frame spectrum. Consider the demands on your time as a factor when choosing a trading style.

- Long-term time-frames

    Long-term position traders sit are in it, as the name suggests, for the long run – months, sometimes year-long duration in the case of extended trend strategies. Traders choosing this time-frame want to take advantage of the prospective of reaping large profit margins. The assumption is that if you properly implement a trend style you stand a better chance of greater earning potential than you would gain in a shorter period.

    One advantage of long-term trading is the relatively less focus required to monitor markets. This feature is countered by the level of patience traders require to remain invested in a trade.

- Medium-term time-frame

    Medium-term trading offers a balance in trade time demands. Trade positions can remain open for a few days to sometimes a few weeks.

- Short-term time-frame

    Scalpers practice short-term trading. Trades are open for a very short space of time – typically within a day – with only minor movements in price change needed. Because multiple trades need to be made in order to turn a profit, traders have to have the time and focus to take advantage here.

There are four common trading styles. These are scalping, day trading (also known as intraday trading), swing trading, and or trend trading (also referred to as longer term position trading). The style you settle on would depend on the type of person you are and what your lifestyle permits. A general overview of the trading style, its principles and benefits, is presented below.

Day trading for beginners

Day trading is the buying and selling of foreign currencies on the same day. It can even involve opening trades multiple times during the span of a day. One of the reasons traders choose day trading is so that they can take advantage of small price movements in the market. While this style can prove to be a profitable style if performed properly, it can also prove risky.

The principles involved in day trading:

- Keep up-to-date on market conditions

- It is essential that day traders do their homework and are continually updated on news and events that affect the currency exchange market.

- Know the amount of money you are willing to lose by setting a risk margin. As a beginner, you will want to risk the smallest margin on your trades.

- Have no limitations on your time

- In order to be a successful day trader, you need to have time available to study the market, explore opportunities and respond promptly to market movements or broker re-quotes. These can happen at any time during open sessions.

Why would you choose Day trading?

The advantages of this trading style include:

- Make as many trades as you want

    You can open and close as many trade positions as you want. The potential to make money quickly (dependent on favorable market factors) is possible.

- The overnight risk is removed

    One of the challenges of holding a trade position open overnight is that there is a higher risk of your trade being affected by dramatic market developments while you are asleep and when you are not able to take the relevant decisions. You have peace of mind.

- Maximize leverage

    Day traders generally make the most of leverage ratios they are offered and with the benefit a low margin. The opportunity of increasing profit is maximized.

- Accelerates trading knowledge and experience

    Day traders gain more experience trading faster in relation to other trading styles as they can open and close more trade positions based on their study of the market conditions.

Day trading does require time, discipline and commitment in order to be a profit-making trading style.

Scalping for beginners

Scalping is recognized as a specialized trading style that offers opportunities to make small gains based on small market price changes usually soon once a trade is entered into and shows profitability. The idea here is to make money by securing more wins in a longer time-frame. Another belief is that the forex market experiences smaller movements more frequently even during quiet times.

The principles involved in scalping

- Quick exit strategy required

    As profits made are small, the potential to lose any gains made in the event of a substantial loss is considerable. One of the underlying expectations that apply to scalping is that the price movement of foreign exchange will move in the desired trend for a short duration, but thereafter the direction onwards remains uncertain – it can drop or rise.

- Many trade positions are required

    As mentioned before, one feature of this trading style is that profits have a small margin; therefore, in order for a trader to make good money, he or she will need to engage in as many trades as possible.

- Discipline is essential

    Scalping is a disciplined trading style that requires traders to make decisions quickly, constantly monitoring the market and have the patience to appreciate small profit margins of each trade.

Why would you choose scalping?

- Risk is limited

    Keeping trade positions open for a brief period reduces exposure to risk. There is less chance of a trade being exposed to negative circumstances.

- Higher frequencies of trade provide greater earnings

    Scalpers can quite easily engage in hundreds of trades over the course of a day with no one trade posing the risk of a big loss. This opens up the potential for big earnings when profits earned are compounded.

- There is always an opportunity for trade

    While some styles are totally dependent on significant movement in the market, this is less so for scalpers. This is because the market is never stagnant; there will always be movement even if it is at a fraction, and that is all the movement that is needed for a scalper.

Scalping is a numbers game, not one dependent on the size of the trade.

Swing trading for beginners

Swing trading is a style suited to traders who can respond promptly to events that affect the market. Traders act quickly to profit from positive swings or if there is a downturn affecting their trade position, they are quick to initiate an exit strategy.

The principles involved in swing trading

- Market volatility required

    Market volatility is an important prerequisite as increases in short-term price moves presents more opportunities to trade.

- Favors technical-based strategies

    Technical traders work within specific parameters that help in their decision-making process of when to open/close trade positions, and risk is limited.

- Larger Stop-Loss orders required

    The fact that swing trading holds trades open for more than one day, in order to limit risk, traders are encouraged to set up larger Stop-Loss orders.

Why would you choose swing trading?

- More trading opportunities

    Seeing that the foreign exchange market is conditioned by a natural cycle (ebb and flow) regular trading opportunities abound. There is a constant change of rising and falling prices to cultivate a favorable environment to buy and sell.

- No need for additional deposit

    Opening and closing positions in a matter of days allows you to identify opportunities for new positions to set up, requiring no deposit between the opening and closing trades.

Swing trading is particularly suited for novice traders as there are plenty of opportunities to trade and positions do not have to be opened for lengthy periods of time, increasing vulnerability to risk due to unforeseen events. Only a reasonable amount of time is required to monitor market activity.

Trend trading for beginners

Trend trading is regarded as one of the simpler styles to operate that offers effective and user-friendly methods to trade successfully. Trending is based on recognizing a trend, opening a trade and exiting once there is a reverse movement on the trend. Trades are held for the long term, a time-frame that allows for larger-than-average returns to be gained. This is the style to adopt if your goal is to reap large yields in profit.

The principles involved in trend trading

- Using tools to identify trends

    Trend traders utilize a number of statistical tools and instruments to identify and benefit from Forex trading. Some of these instruments include charts, technical indicators and

- Designed to generate wealth

    Trend trading offers the most risk-reducing approach to building wealth in the Forex market. Recognize a trend early, hold your position for a time and once you detect a reverse in the trend, exit quickly.

Why would you choose trend trading?

- Large profit margins without minute-by-minute market monitoring

    This trading style doesn't require an intense focus on the market, yet the returns are greater than the norm.

- Fewer transaction costs

    As a trend trader, you be engaged in fewer trades than a day trader. This means that with the fewer trade positions are less transaction costs that need to be paid.

Accurate analysis of market movement, discipline, determination and patience are strong requirements to reap the rewards of trend trading.

Trading strategies and approaches

You don't need complicated complex strategies to win at Forex trading. Sometimes the simpler strategies triumph over complex ones. Find strategies you are comfortable with and that works for you and stick with those.

The next step is to choose a strategy that will allow you to make money from your trades at minimum risk to you. Once you have a strategy defined the next recommended advice is to practice, practice, practice before you invest any real money in it.

Various types of strategies

In Forex trading strategies are used to help traders make certain decisions like when to open a trade when to close a position as well as how to how to enter and exit a trade. Strategies can make use of a number of analytical and statistical tools and information-gathering methodologies. As the Forex market is a dynamic one, and with new innovations and developments in digital technology, trading strategies are updated to allow for improved analytical methods to support traders in their profit-making goals.

Fundamental analysis

The fundamental analysis strategy investigates the influence of major economic and political indicators that contribute to a currency's demand and supply, and which in return influences the currency exchange rate.

In dealing with economic indicators and other variables it is to be expected that this strategy is often experienced as tricky and complex to work with. Current news and data releases are some of the major sources of essential information.

Technical analysis

Technical analysis is another basic main artery of Foreign exchange trading strategies that are popular with many traders. This strategy is based on studying both past and the latest movements in currency prices. Information is plotted on charts which are then closely analyzed to ascertain onward movement. The reasoning behind this strategy is that market movement primarily decided by forces such as demand and supply that sets out the margins for increase or decrease in exchange rates. In using technical analysis, traders are provided with a scientific basis for engaging in a trade, making decision-making more concrete.

Range trading

This is a simple trading strategy that works on the principle that currency prices can maintain stability within a specified high and low range for a certain period of time. This holds true especially for currencies that are rarely manipulated by unforeseen events. The promise of predictability is a favorable factor here.

Momentum trading

Momentum trading is founded on the idea that the force of significant price movements along a specific course is a good indication that this price movement will likely proceed on this course. This strategy also takes into consideration that trends may weaken, indicating a reversal. Factors such as price and volume are critical here as is utilizing graphical instruments like candlestick charts.

An important note on trading strategies

As you have seen from the above there are a great many diverse approaches to trading in foreign currency. These work by understanding movements in price and how to profit from them. While you may find that relying on one specific strategy is simpler, no one strategy will be profitable all the time. It is suggested that you create your own hybrid version by using the complementary features of various strategies. As you are about to enter a market has is constantly changing, it is important for you to learn to adapt to these changes by having an array of resources available.

How to develop your own Forex trading strategy

At some point along your path, you may discover that you want to build your own trading strategy. What follows is a step-by-step guide to creating your own exclusive strategy to making money from currency trading.

Step 1: Decide on your time-frame

You first need to establish your trading style and the time-frame that best fits in with your goals and lifestyle. Do you have the time and are you willing to monitor the market and pore over technical data daily or weekly? How long are you willing to keep trade positions open? The time-frame you choose will determine the type of strategy you want to create. Don't be afraid to play around, at first, with numerous time-frames before you settle on a particular one.

Step 2: Decide on the indicators you will use

Indicators are data points used to help traders spot trading trends and provide them with essential information with which to optimize a trade approach. These data points tie in closely with the time-frame a trader chooses for a trade. There are a number of indicators you can use; one of the more widely used is moving averages. Others include Momentum Oscillators, Bollinger Band and RSI. Once again, your trading style will determine which indicators you decide on.

Step 3: Include indicators that verify trends

There is a phenomenon in the Forex market termed "False trends'. This trend is based on false signals that provide an inaccurate representation of economic reality. Various market factors may create a false trend, some of these are timing lags, anomalies in data sources and algorithms. Having indicators to verify or affirm a trend is useful in protecting your trade from unsuspected loss.

Step 4: Decide on how much you are prepared to lose

Considering and defining an amount you are willing to risk on a trade is an important step that many traders overlook. Trading is a two-way street and you can as easily make money as you can lose it. The benefit of deciding on a particular amount is that you can exit a trade as soon as you see the market is not moving in your favor and you lose only that specified amount and not all of your capital. Your risk management technique is an influential factor in how successful you are as a trader.

Step 5: Determine entry and exit points

The entry and exit points you choose to trade with contribute to the profitability of your trade. In determining these points, you will refer to the information provided by the indicator you have chosen for your strategy. If the indicators point to favorable market conditions you may take this as a good signal to enter. Exit points can be decided on various factors. An example of a simple exit point strategy is deciding on a set target. Once the currency exchange price meets that target, you exit the trade. Another exit point technique is to select various factors that will indicate it is time to close a trade.

Step 6: Set out strategy rules

Creating your own trading strategy is not about breaking rules but sticking to them. As part of your step-by-step guide to creating your very own exclusive strategy is taking the time to set out and WRITE DOWN rules for yourself. One of the main determinants of a successful trader is discipline. Unless you stick to the rules you cannot expect your system to generate a profit for you.

No system will ever work for you if you don't stick to the rules, so remember to be disciplined.

Step 7: Test, test, test

Once you have worked out the workings of your strategy, it is time to test it to find out how well it works or to fine tune it and address the kinks. Testing your strategy can be done through a charting software product – one of the quicker ways to test strategy viability. A second method is to practice on a demo account. Honesty about wins and losses is critically important.

How long you test your strategy is up to you, but you should realistically give back testing two months. If you maintain good results consistently for a period of time (once again this is up to you) you can then take the next leap forward and go live. Just remember to take a deep breath first.

The role of Forex indicator in enhancing trading strategy

Forex indicators are especially useful data points that point to the direction or trend in which a particular currency will proceed. Traders use these indicators to gain insight into the market and to improve the profitability of the trading strategies they wish to implement. Indicators can be used in conjunction with any trading style, strategy or time-frame. The trick with Forex indicators is to select the right complement that affirms each other for accurate strategy development. The indicators traders choose must choose the right combination that will help them in profiteering in a fast-moving, fast-changing market.

Different types of indicators

There are a number of different types of indicators that may make choosing the right ones a challenge. Generally, there are two main branches of Forex indicators:

Leading technical indicators

Indicators under this grouping point to possible market movement based on the route a specific currency pair takes or ultimate position a currency pair would attain.

Lagging technical indicators

Indicators under these grouping assist traders in being updated on the latest market movements. Traders use information from these data points to ascertain whether market trends proceeds in a sideways direction or up or down.

7 Important Forex indicators to consider are:

1. Simple Moving Averages

Simple Moving Averages points to the average currency rate for a specified duration (10 minutes, 30 minutes or a day). Each time frame carries the same weight.

2. Exponential Moving Average

The averages, under this indictor, are determined using latest Forex rates that hold a higher weighting in the total average. Traders use this indicator to gain a more precise indication of the market trend direction.

3. Relative Strength Index

This indicator works with a range between 0-100. In using the RSI traders try to spot a point of deviation at which a rate reaches a new high without the RSI exceeding an earlier high. This point of deviation may indicate an imminent reversal. The RSI is widely used by day traders to measure currency price's gains and losses.

4. Moving Average Convergence/Divergence (MACD)

The MACD indicator is based on the charting of two momentum lines. The MACD line is the distinction between two exponential moving averages and the signal line.

5. Stochastic Oscillator

This indicator points to short-term exaggerated buying and selling conditions ranging on a scale of 0%-100%. The Stochastic Oscillator takes into account in the event of uptrend closing rates for specified durations are more intense in the top half of the period's range. The opposite is true for a downward trend where closing rates are focused in the lower half of the range.

6. Bollinger Bands

Bollinger bands are comprised of three lines: the moving average, an upper line, and a lower line. These lines point to the movement of price rate increases and decreases from the averages identified. A price rate that is below the lower line shows potential for a future increase while a price rate that is placed above the upper line, it may indicate a favorable time to sell.

7. Momentum Oscillators

The momentum oscillator indicator is used when a trader wants to establish whether a price rate will increase or decrease. The indicator makes it easy for traders to spot imminent market movement. If the currency rate attains a landmark high while the oscillator is not at the same level, this may indicate a gradual decrease in demand followed by a drop-in price rate.

The ultimate goal of Forex indicators is to assist traders to gain a better understanding of market activity which will allow them to make informed decisions in regard to the trades they enter and exit. The above indicators are by no means the full complement of indicators used by traders, but they do form a good list with which to formulate winning strategies.

Chapter 6

Choosing a forex broker - step-by-step guide

Forex brokers make available a number of Forex trade tools to help you along your path to currency trade success. These can take the form of real-time charts, economic calendars, current affairs, data analysis and other technical analysis in real-time as well as user support for products such as trading systems. As a beginner, you want to take advantage of all resources at your disposal to help you succeed at your Forex goals.

How to choose your forex broker

1. Find a Forex broker

When choosing your Forex broker, make certain that they have the necessary credentials and registered with the relevant bodies such as the Futures Commission Merchant (FCM) and governed by Commodity Futures Trading Commission (CFTC). Such credentials point to brokers meeting ethical and financial standards. Furthermore, they are more likely to offer a better level of transparency in their operations.

For extra peace of mind, you can also check the National Futures Association Background Affiliation Status Information Center (BASIC) website to find out whether your chosen brokerage company had any official proceedings (issues with clients or authority bodies) against it.

Large and established brokerage companies have the resources (employees, top digital systems) to provide proper support and stability during times of heightened market activity.

Forex brokers are in abundant supply and not all are created equal, so how do you choose one from the other when shopping around for your ideal broker? One broker may offer high leverage ratios? Others may have user-friendly trading platforms or attractive spreads. A good piece of advice is to have a list of questions on hand to help better judge which broker has all the necessary requirements to suit your needs. Use this list as a point of reference:

- Is the broker well financed?
- How long has the broker been established?
- How many clients does the broker have?
- Who manages the company and how much experience does this person have?
- How many banks has the broker established relationships with? And with which ones?
- What is the volume of its monthly transactions?
- What back-end office functions does the broker offer in real time?
- What method is used to obtain pricing?

- What are the broker's trading costs (commissions, markups, margin costs, etc.)?
- What trading restrictions apply?

2. Trial test software platforms and systems

Look for brokers that offer free trials so that you can test the various trading platforms before you select the right broker to help you succeed at your Forex trading goals. You can do this by opening a demo account (or multiple demo accounts with different brokers) and practice trading with virtual currency. This will help give you a feel for Forex trading and become familiar with using the trading platform. Demo accounts mirror live accounts as they usually offer the same functionalities and with market prices in real time.

3. Find relevant research resources

Information is king, particularly in Forex trading. Even your practice runs on demo accounts require you to do proper research before you engage in a trade. You have to become adept at rationalizing a trade. Remember the Forex market is largely a technical one. The best experienced traders know the advantage of being informed about the market and the daily need to be updated on important national and global developments. Newspapers and Forex-centered websites can prove especially useful.

Chapter 7

The purpose of demo accounts

Every beginner trader is offered one major piece of advice – practice on demo trading first before entering a live trade in real time and with real money. Novices should try their hand at demo trading from anywhere between two and six months. When you trade live you enter a market dominated by experts and experienced professional traders, so it is best to practice strategies, time-frames, learn how to use Forex instruments accurately and test entry and exit points.

Your guide to Demo accounts

The learning curve of trading can be very steep and if you are just starting out then you should really consider starting out trading with a demo account.

Starting out as a beginner trader, no matter how excited you are, can be overwhelming. If the many concepts and terms to wrap your head around is not enough, there is the forex market itself and related influential factors to understand. Every beginner stares at a vertical learning curve before them. Mistakes are a natural part of such a dynamic trading platform. So then how do you give yourself the best chance of success in the face of substantial odd?

Fortunately, and thanks to digital technology, beginner traders can choose to gain valuable trading experience through demo accounts. Demo accounts are free trading accounts provided by broker companies that make use of virtual money. Novice traders can learn about buying and selling foreign currency, and how the Forex market works without putting up or losing any real money.

Another great benefit of demo accounts is that you are provided with access to a complete range of trade tools and vital platform features to try out like the all-important Stop-Loss and Limit-Order strategies.

Depending on the broker you choose, you are offered practice on demo accounts for an unlimited amount of time while some brokers only allow demo accounts to be open within a restricted timeframe.

Why you should open a demo account first

A demo account is the best and most popular way to teach yourself how to trade in the Forex market at no cost or risk to your precious capital. You use a demo account to implement different strategies, learn the advantages and disadvantages of each to find the best ones for your goals. Once you have selected a strategy, opened a position and closed the order, you can review how you fared. Important lessons can be learned in this way.

How to use simulated demo accounts effectively?

If the point and purpose of a simulated trading account is to teach beginner traders to become profitable at Forex trading, it is important that you gain maximum benefit from them.

- Understanding the Trading Platform

Use demo accounts for the purpose that they were created for. One of these purposes is to gain an understanding of the Forex trading platform they will use to buy and sell currencies. You will learn how orders are executed when to use different types of orders effectively and which risk management techniques are ideal for you. Think of the trading platform like you would a teacher that best explains, in a practical way, how to use Forex tools and indicators, charting tools and analysis tools.

- Resource tools

    Some brokers offer wonderful sources of vital information on the demo accounts they provide. These important sources of information in the form of a news bar can relate to Technical and Fundamental Analysis, which when used properly can result in profitable trades.

- Create a powerful marketing tool for other traders

    While this is not strictly a primary benefit of demo accounts, it is another way of monetizing your skill, knowledge and experience for the benefit of other traders. This takes the form of selling subscriptions to proven forex trading signals and alerts that you have developed and know works well. You can use your demo account as a convincing track record of signals used to generate winning trades.

Step-by-step guide to getting started with a demo account

While it may be that you are only practicing trading with virtual money, it is important that you take these practice runs seriously. See your demo account as if it is an actual live one and the virtual money as 'real'.

Step1

Determine the amount of money you have to open your demo account (this should be the same amount that you have to fund your real live account). Even during these trial trade sessions, it is important that you apply the same level of excitement and motivation that you would as if you are actually trading. You should mirror your simulated trading world to reflect your real-time one.

Step 2

With an opened demo account, you can then begin to speculate on the market and buy and sell currency. You get to experience the trading platform and learn what each feature does. This is not the time to shy away from making mistakes as there is nothing to lose, only valuable lessons and prized experience to gain.

Step 3

Once you've 'played' around on the virtual platform for a while, you can then begin to try out different strategies to find the one that fits your personality, risk profile and goals best. Start out with a few basics ones like day trading or swing trading before you move on to more complex strategies like fundamental analysis.

Step 4

Live trading in real time. Once you have begun to make consistent gains in virtual trading and you feel comfortable with the whole process it is generally regarded that you are ready for real live trading and move onto an actual account. You are still advised to tread cautiously and start off with minimal amounts. Your practice runs are just that, practice with no real risk to your own money.

Before trading with your own money, have you:

- Established risk management techniques such as Stop-Loss orders or No negative balance orders?

- Have you perfected your strategy system and know it well?

- Refrained from making impulsive trades?

- Gained a solid understanding of the nature of the Forex market and the terms used in trading?

Chapter 8

Step by Step Guide for Opening your First Live Forex Trading Position

So, you have mastered demo trading. You have tested the advantages and benefits provided by more than one broker trading platform. Having experienced different broker companies and how they work, you now have a good idea of which broker to choose from.

Opening a forex trading account and trading live is easy and simple and involves the following main steps:

1. You are selecting an account type
2. You enter the registration details required
3. You activate your account

Step 1: Selecting an account type

Once you are ready to trade live and with real money, you have to decide on the type of foreign exchange trading account you want to open. Traders can opt for either a personal account or corporate account. Remember that as you will be trading on this broker's platform and trading in real-time involves using your own money, it is important that you read the terms and conditions very carefully before signing up.

Depending on your broker of choice you may be offered a "managed account" option. This type of account allows your broker to buy and sell on your account on your behalf. Managed accounts come with a price tag attached – a larger minimum deposit is required to open one and the broker managing the account will be due to his managing 'fee' so take this into consideration. Beginner Forex traders are advised to opt for a spot account instead of other types such as forwards or futures account.

Speaking of costs, make sure you are aware of all the relevant fees and costs your broker charges. One often overlooked cost is the fee charged for bank wire transfers. These can be hefty and eat into your profits so factor it in when selecting your broker.

Step 3: Activate your account

After receiving your registration forms, your broker will send an email with further instructions on how to activate your account. Once you have followed the account activation instructions, a final email follows providing you with your username and password.

After these steps have been successfully completed, you will receive a final email with your username, password, and instructions on how to fund your account.

After these steps have been completed, you will receive a final email with your username, password, and instructions on how to deposit capital into your account.

Step by Step Guide for Opening your First Live Forex Trading Position

With an account all set up and funded, you are good to go and enter your first trade.

BUT WAIT! Before you do that, let's review a few basic rules first.

It is par for the course should you have anxious feelings about your first live Forex trade. After all, this is no simulation practice and you will be risking real money. In a real money setup, you will have to rule out emotion, respond promptly to re-quotes and movements in the market

No matter how practiced you are the enormity of the occasion means there is the possibility of mistakes being made. It is not uncommon for traders to choose the wrong order type or choose the wrong lot size. Your first live trade position is still regarded as a practical learning session. Take note of the following:

Rule 1

Know your trading platform thoroughly. Know how to open a position – what buttons to click on to execute orders, what each feature represents and why you have made certain selections – like you would know the back of your hand.

Rule 2

Have you a solid grasp of why you should implement a risk management strategy? Do you know how to use accurate position size for your position?

Rule 3

If mistakes are made or loss suffered, take the lesson and move on. You will need to learn how to react positively and recover from a loss. If you make a profit, use the take profit strategy to your advantage.

Rule 4

Once your trade position has closed, review the decisions you took with your first live Forex trade. Were you successful? What contributed to its success? Did you have a proper strategy and risk management technique in place or was it just a good guess? Did you suffer a loss? Can you identify where you went wrong?

Remember your first live position is still a lesson in learning. That is the ultimate point of a first trade so try not to focus too much whether you made a profit or loss. A win can provide a false sense of security only for you to make mistakes that are far costlier down the road. Focusing on a loss and not learning where things went wrong will end your career hopes as a trader before you even got started.

Chapter 9

Risk management – How to minimize risk and maximize rewards

It is generally understood that in order to derive massive gains you need to take greater risks. Not so for someone just starting out in Forex trading. Remember you are in it for the long haul and small incremental gains is the surefire way to building confidence and proven trading strategies.

Risk management is all about minimizing your losses when trading in currencies. As discussed before the Forex market is a highly volatile one and you can make a good profit as well as experience heavy losses.

Before you plunge headfirst into making a trade it is critical that you ascertain risk and investigate ways to manage that risk. Trading without risk management draws a thin line between trading and gambling.

Risk management is firstly a form of protection. Secondly controlling losses in the long-term enables profit-building.

So, how do you trade with the goal of making money with the least amount of risk? Remember the first rule of thumb is to set a limit of the amount of actual money you are prepared to lose.

Here are a number of additional risk-limiting techniques to consider as an essential part of your trading strategies:

- Set up Stop-Loss orders

    This is the oft-referred to absolute technique to avoid unlimited risk and should be at the top of every beginner's risk management plan. You determine your trade's risk margin (you cap the amount you are prepared to lose) without impeding potential profit. Industry experts encourage you to ensure you have this type of order set up for every open trade position. A Stop-Loss order does as its name suggests, it stops your account from suffering further loss.

- Limit position size and leverage ratios

    Position size is linked to exposed risk. The larger the position size and higher leverage ratios, the higher the increase in risk factor. Trading in this situation and your position is vulnerable to routine negative price changes. Remember that even if your Forex broker offers you a high leverage ratio, it does not mean you have to use it. You have the option to ask for a lower leverage ratio.

- Establish a comprehensive trade plan

    Having a well-thought out trade plan established for every open position is one of the more effective ways to limit risk. Not only would you use one if you have it set up, you also avoid trade mistakes such as overtrading or making impulsive trades.

- Stay informed and updated on what's happening in the market

  This risk management technique is especially important for currency pair pertinent to your trade. Are there any data and events that are timetabled close to your trade plans? By being aware of market conditions by no means guarantees you making a profit but at the very least you can take into consideration adverse circumstances and take the necessary steps to protect your risk as best as possible.

- Be particular about when you trade

  It is advisable that you choose the times you trade wisely. You don't have to be at it 24 hours a day. Not every session presents the best time in which to trade. Rather take advantage of trades that offer clear-cut risk/rewards opportunities.

- Become proficient in distinguishing the characteristics that define different currency pairing

  There are numerous factors that come into play when trading in specific currency pairs and that varies your position's vulnerability to risk. The dynamic nature of each currency pairing and the level of risk attached necessitates that you have different trade strategies applicable to each pair.

Not having a risk management plan in place opens you up to not only losing money you can't afford to lose but, it also lowers your confidence level, your motivation to stay in the game and increases the possibility of you making further mistakes.

Chapter 10

The important role of Forex research

Let's face it. Research is time-consuming and requires your focus and effort. Unless you're an academician do you really need to spend all that time and energy that you could be spending on practicing trade techniques? Yes, if you want to be a success at Forex trading and earn the big money.

Forex trading is a highly competitive challenging market to trade in. Any trader worth his or her salt knows the plus-points of using research and information for profitable trading.

Essentially research is information-gathering and speculating and trading in the currency exchange market is built on the information you have. Whether you are a novice preparing for your first trade or a seasoned trader, one of your core activities will be research. This is not one of those steps you will want to miss.

As a beginner, your goal is to gain a better understanding of the different elements that make up the foreign exchange market, the intricacies of Forex trading and the different strategies a trader can employ.

Armed with the relevant and accurate information you are better prepared to capitalize on profit-making opportunities and take appropriate precautionary measures to decrease the level of potential loss. Remember you need up-to-date facts and figures on trends, events, and patterns to make informed trading decisions.

Technical analysis and Fundamental analysis have a dual role to play in Forex trading. They double as both effective trading strategies and information-gathering methodologies. While there are any number of ways to gain the information you need, these two analytical methods are reputed to be the best and most widely-used. Both approaches depend on market trends past and present) to decide on prospective patterns. There are particular advantages and disadvantages to using each methodology, so it is advised to consider the merits of each one for your particular trade.

Relevant research provides a Forex trader with firstly, analytical information with which to make accurate predictions that determine the direction and movement of currency exchange rates and make trade decisions based on them.

Secondly, there many different currency pairs with which to engage in buying and selling. Research provides you with an overview of rewarding currency pairs and by charting data accurately, you have a better idea of when to enter a trade or close an order.

A note of caution.

Research is an undeniably critical part of Forex trading but like all tools, it is how you use it to your advantage that is important and a determinant to your success.

Conclusion

Thank for making it through to the end of *Forex Trading for Beginners*, let's hope it was informative and able to provide you with all of the tools you need to achieve your goals whatever they may be.

The next step is to set out your very own plan of action. Register for a demo account or two. Choose an established strategy or develop one of your own. Then try your hand at earning a virtual profit with virtual funds on a virtual trading platform, all at no cost to you but with gaining invaluable practical experience. After a few months, you have gained the confidence needed to trade in real-time, you are ready to set up your live account.

Before you go, review these top 11 tips to avoid trade disasters.

1. Learn the basics

    After reading this book you can tick this one off your list.

2. Self-awareness

    Know thyself has never been more applicable than to a Forex trader. Know what your needs are, what your goals are and what your risk tolerance is.

3. Commit to your plan

    There is a reason why sticking to your trade plan is important. Forex trading requires patience and discipline. With a demo account, this is easy to do as there is no real risk to you. With practice discipline becomes habitual – you do it without even thinking about it.

4. Deciding on a broker requires careful consideration

    Much depends on the broker you choose. The advantages of their products and services, related costs and level of support are all important factors a beginner trader has to consider.

5. Begin small

    One of the biggest mistakes novice traders make is to aim for substantial rewards. In beginning small opt for lo leverage ratios and be happy with small consistent gains.

6. Trade in a single currency pair before moving on to more complex trades

    Beginner traders find keeping on top of all the different aspects that goes into a trade somewhat challenging. It is therefore suggested to concentrate on trading in just one currency pair with which to gain a feel for the market and build skills.

7. Act only when you're confident

    Having the confidence to trade means that you need to understand and be willing to accept the consequences, both positive and negative. Avoid acting on rumors or when you're unsure.

Conclusion

8. Limit the influence of your emotions

    Emotions should be ruled out of Forex trading strategies. While you cannot get rid of emotion completely (it is part of being human) you can limit its influence on your decision making. Small-scale trades mean the risk is small and there is less opportunity to allow emotions to come to the fore. Lots of trading practice is another effective way to sideline emotion.

9. Don't trust in magical methods and formulas

    Like with all trades there is no magic formula for success. Success begins and ends with determination and commitment. Be wary of products and services that guarantee fantastic profit margins and immediate success.

10. Don't trade against market trends

    This is a definite no-no for novice traders. By following trends, you eliminate the stress and angst that only come with betting against market movement.

11. Persist in attaining your goals

    Yes, another reminder to be determined is required. It is that important. This is a key that unlocks the door to success. Developing skills and experience does not happen overnight.

Success at Forex trading can be likened to a marathon race in which slow and steady wins the race!

Finally, if you found this book useful in any way, a review on Amazon is always appreciated!

www.ingramcontent.com/pod-product-compliance
Lightning Source LLC
Chambersburg PA
CBHW052339220526
45472CB00001B/499